AMAZING MILITARY FACTS

AMAZING
U.S. AIR FORCE
FACTS

by Mandy R. Marx

CAPSTONE PRESS
a capstone imprint

Pebble Plus is published by Capstone Press,
1710 Roe Crest Drive, North Mankato, Minnesota 56003
www.mycapstone.com

Library of Congress Cataloging-in-Publication Data
Names: Marx, Mandy R., author.
Title: Amazing U.S. Air Force facts / by Mandy R. Marx.
Other titles: Amazing United States Air Force facts
Description: North Mankato, Minnesota : Capstone Press, 2017. | Series:
  Pebble plus. Amazing military facts | Includes bibliographical references
  and index. | Audience: Age 4-8. | Audience: Grades K-3.
Identifiers: LCCN 2016016907| ISBN 9781515709510 (library binding) |
ISBN 9781515709831 (pbk.) | ISBN 9781515711186 (ebook (pdf)
Subjects: LCSH: United States. Air Force—Juvenile literature.
Classification: LCC UG633 .M3149 2017 | DDC 358.400973—dc23
LC record available at https://lccn.loc.gov/2016016907

Editorial Credits
Kayla Rossow, designer; Jo Miller, media researcher; Kathy McColley, production specialist

Photo Credits
Getty Images: USAF, 21; Shutterstock: Elena Elisseeva, 23, 24; U.S. Air Force courtesy graphic, 7;
U.S. Air Force photo by Airman 1st Class Daniel Phelps, 9, Airman 1st Class Shawna L. Keyes, 17,
Airman 1st Class Tryphena Mayhugh, 5, Senior Airman Christine Griffiths, cover, Senior Airman
Julianne Showalter, 14, Senior Airman Nadine Y. Barclay, 15, Staff Sgt. Aaron Allmon, 19,
Staff Sgt. Douglas Ellis, 13, Tech. Sgt. Justin D. Pyle, 1, Tech. Sgt. Manuel J. Martinez, 11

Note to Parents and Teachers

The Amazing Military Facts set supports national curriculum standards for science related
to science, technology, and society. This book describes and illustrates amazing facts about
the United States Air Force. The images support early readers in understanding the text.
The repetition of words and phrases helps early readers learn new words. This book
also introduces early readers to subject-specific vocabulary words, which are defined in
the Glossary section. Early readers may need assistance to read some words and to use
the Table of Contents, Glossary, Read More, Internet Sites, Critical Thinking Using the
Common Core, and Index sections of the book.

Printed and bound in the USA.
009655F16

Table of Contents

Amazing Airmen Facts

Members of the U.S. Air Force are called airmen. Women are called airmen too. In 2013 about one-fifth of airmen were women.

The Air Force has 86 bases.

Airmen do different jobs at each base.

Eglin Air Force Base is in Florida.

Airmen there track 20,000 objects in space.

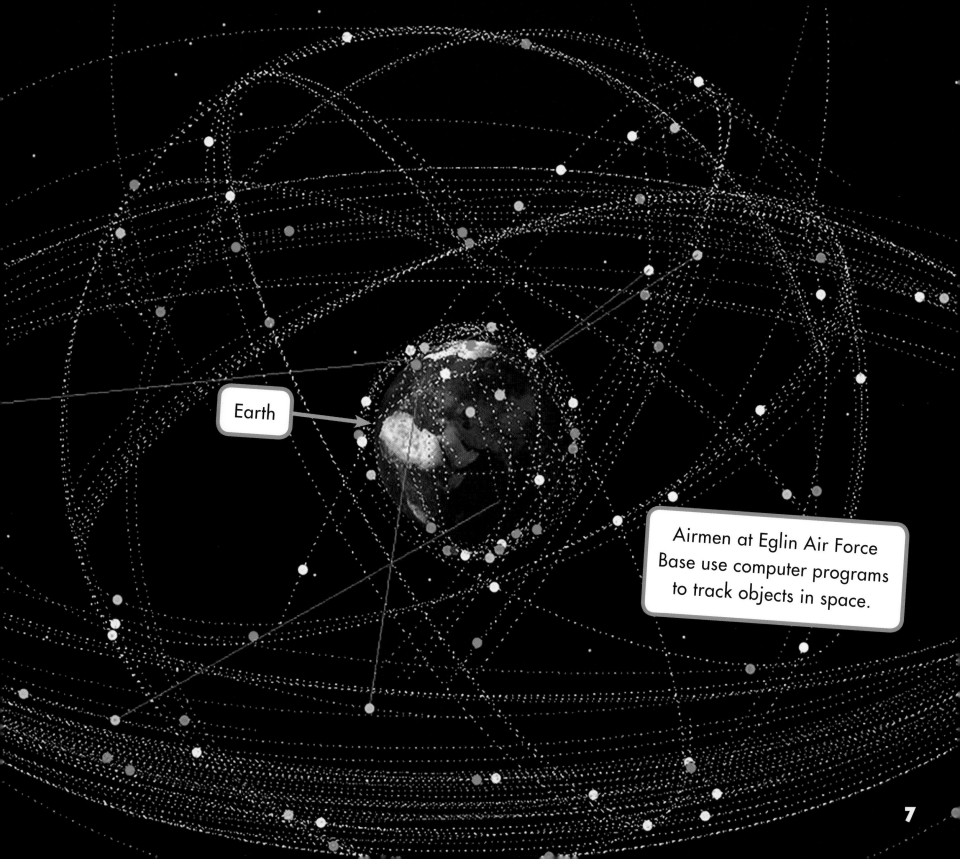

Earth

Airmen at Eglin Air Force Base use computer programs to track objects in space.

Amazing On-the-Job Facts

Each year about 1,000 airmen become pilots. Before they can be pilots, they go through training. Training lasts 240 days.

The Thunderbirds put on air shows. They fly fast jets. The jets move in patterns. They can fly just 18 inches (46 centimeters) apart.

Some Special Forces airmen fly into dangerous places. They jump from airplanes. These airmen rescue people.

Amazing Vehicle Facts

Some airmen fly drones.

These planes have no pilots.

The airmen sit at computers.

They use joysticks to control drones.

Air Force jets are fast! Some fly 1,500 miles (2,414 kilometers) per hour. They can cross the United States in less than three hours.

Amazing Weapons Facts

Some jets carry lots of weapons.

The A-10 Thunderbolt II can hold

16,000 pounds (7,257 kilograms).

That's as heavy as an African elephant.

Some missiles hit targets 6,000 miles (9,700 km) away. That's like flying from California to China.

Glossary

airman—a person in the Air Force

base—an area run by the military where people serving in the military live and military supplies are stored

drone—an unmanned aircraft that is controlled from the ground

jet—an engine that uses streams of hot gas to make power

joystick—a control stick

missile—an explosive weapon that is thrown or shot at a distant target from a ship or from the ground

pilot—a person who flies a jet or plane

target—an object at which to aim or shoot

Read More

Abramovitz, Melissa. *Military Trucks.* Military Machines. North Mankato, Minn.: Capstone Press, 2012.

Collard, Sneed B. *U.S. Air Force: Absolute Air Power.* Freedom Forces. Vero Beach, Fla.: Rourke Educational Media, 2013.

Murray, Julie. *United States Air Force.* U.S. Armed Forces. Minneapolis: Abdo Kids, 2015.

Internet Sites

FactHound offers a safe, fun way to find Internet sites related to this book. All of the sites on FactHound have been researched by our staff.

Here's all you do:

Visit *www.facthound.com*

Type in this code: 9781515709510

Super-cool stuff!

Check out projects, games and lots more at
www.capstonekids.com

Critical Thinking
Using the Common Core

1. Why do you think airmen track objects in space? (Integration of Knowledge and Ideas)

2. What is one benefit of a drone compared to a jet or an airplane? (Key Ideas and Details)

Index